Diccon Bewes and Michael Meister

False Friends

51 Ways to Be Misunderstood

Dicam Bewes

M. Meister

Bergli

Diccon Bewes has lived in Switzerland for ten years and is author of *Swiss Watching* and *Slow Train to Switzerland*.

Michael Meister is a Swiss illustrator and cartoonist, who draws for companies and newspapers from Hong Kong to Zurich to New York.

better an honest
enemy than
a false friend

Learning a foreign language isn't always easy. You make mistakes and embarrass yourself every day, often thanks to false friends. These are the words that look like ones you know but mean something completely different. They aren't the worst part of learning another language but they're often the funniest.

We both found that out the hard way. Michael thinks in Swiss German while trying to speak English, whereas Diccon is an English speaker trying to think in German; somewhere in the middle we manage to communicate, though when it comes to false friends neither of us is ever totally sure what the other really means.

If Michael says mist, is he swearing or commenting on the weather? When Diccon asks for the menu, is he very hungry or trying to save money? It's these moments of mutual misunderstanding that make learning another language embarrassing and entertaining in equal measure. Once you've said Präservativ instead of preservative, you'll never make that mistake again – and you'll have added to your vocabulary.

With this selection of our favourite false friends, we hope to save you from a few blushes and blunders. Some words you might already know (or think you do), others might surprise you, but they all want to deceive you so none can be trusted. Not least because false friends come in a variety of disguises.

There are those that hide in plain sight by taking the form of an identical word but with a completely different meaning: a gift is welcome in English but definitely not in German. Then there are loan words, stolen from other languages. English and German both took chef from French but one left him in an office, the other put him in a kitchen.

Perhaps the most cunning are those that pretend to follow the rules, and then lead you astray. If bringen means to bring then surely it's only logical that winken means to wink. You know that Liebe is love, so beliebt must be beloved, right?

A few of our false friends may have you nodding in ashamed agreement, as you recall making exactly the same mistake. Some might also have you scratching your head as you try to solve the puzzle of which word is playing tricks with you. There is a glossary at the back to explain each of the false friends.

Most of all, we hope all our cartoons will leave you laughing and let you enjoy these false friends as much as we do. Whether you're learning English or German, they are a language's way of reminding us who's in charge.

Diccon Bewes and Michael Meister

No one trusted Andreas because he always had a hidden agenda.

"And remember, children, this is NOT an angel!"

Today Roger had to play a real tennis ass.

"I need a beamer for my presentation."

My husband becomes a present every Christmas.

The senator was beloved, especially among male voters.

A monk should bet five times a day.

Uncle Max always gets drunk at parties and blames his wife.

Magellan was the first man to sail around the world in a boot.

The designer accidentally created a new brand.

Every week Rob got briefs from home.

His bureau has just enough room for him and a secretary.

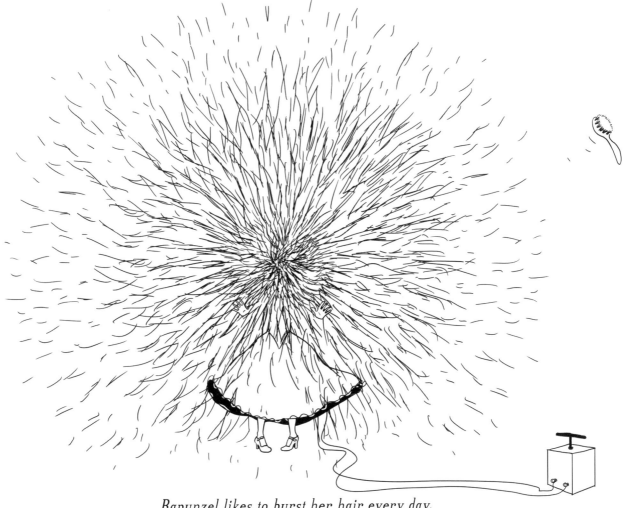

Rapunzel likes to burst her hair every day.

"Honey, maybe next time we should hire a stretch limo?"

"I'm a bit scared of my chef."

"For the last time, what is your confession?"

Maggie likes her customers to be very devout.

Little Heidi was so ill the doctor gave her a double dose.

"Well, I am a very engaged employee."

Sadly, Karl has to work in a very ugly fabric.

"Please complete this formula, sir."

I bought my mother-in-law a special gift for her birthday.

Four years at the local gymnasium didn't produce the results Markus expected.

Christina has a new ceramic herd in her kitchen.

Jack needed a bigger hose.

Beatrice always wears a hut when she is sunbathing.

Once the lager was open, Bob and Ted couldn't leave.

The children dreaded it being father's turn for the lecture at bedtime.

Golf was invented in Scotland, which is why a golf course has 18 lochs.

A British banker always used to wear a melon to work.

"He ordered the WHOLE MENU!"

"*This is our famous middle-aged fountain.*"

He couldn't see anything in the mist.

Doris loved polishing her old timer.

Poor old John has a very small pension.

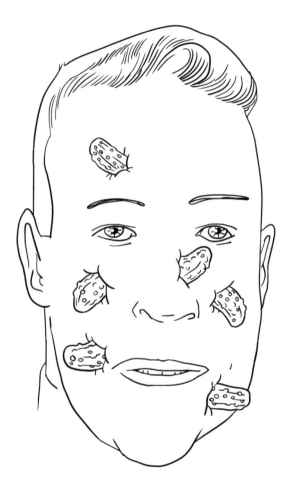

Teenage boys often suffer from pickles on their faces.

The key to being a successful salesman is to be pregnant.

"Preservatives help some things last longer."

After two puffs he was out of breath.

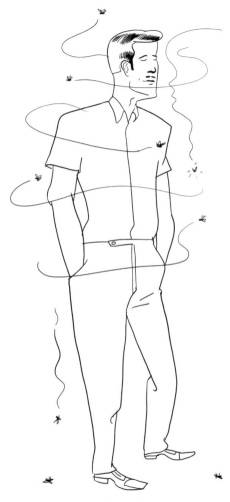

Leo was tall, rank and handsome.

The depressed cat needed some rat.

Betty liked to take a Roman to bed with her.

"Sorry, sir, no smoking."

They stick together.

My wife gave me two tablets for my headache.

Peter loves to taste his new computer.

Blackbeard sat on his treasure to keep it safe.

"Last year I went on holiday in the Turkey."

Swiss voters go to the urn every few months.

"Mirror, mirror on the wand..."

The Queen always winks at the crowd.

Glossary

The English version of the false friend always appears first.

Agenda
No one trusted Andreas because he always had a hidden agenda.
An agenda is a list of things to do (die Tagesordnung);
a hidden agenda is an ulterior motive (der Hintergedanke).
Die Agenda means a diary or in American English a datebook.

Angel
"And remember, children, this is NOT an angel!"
An angel is a heavenly messenger (der Engel).
Die Angel means a fishing rod.

Ass
Today Roger had to play a real tennis ass.
An ass is a donkey (der Esel) or in American English a bottom (der Arsch).
Das Ass is an ace, either in cards or in sport.

Beamer
"I need a beamer for my presentation."
A beamer (also beemer) is slang for a BMW car (der BMW).
Der Beamer means a projector.

Become
My husband becomes a present every Christmas.
To become is to change into or grow into (werden).
Bekommen means to get or to receive.

Beloved	*The senator was beloved, especially among male voters.* Beloved is to be much loved (geliebt). Beliebt means popular.
Bet	*A monk should bet five times a day.* To bet is to gamble (wetten). Beten means to pray.
Blame	*Uncle Max always gets drunk at parties and blames his wife.* To blame is to declare someone responsible for a fault or wrong (die Schuld geben). Blamieren means to embarrass.
Boot	*Magellan was the first man to sail around the world in a boot.* A boot is a type of footwear (der Stiefel). Das Boot means a boat.
Brand	*The designer accidentally created a new brand.* A brand is a product's official name or trademark (die Marke). Der Brand means a fire.
Briefs	*Every week Rob got briefs from home.* Briefs are men's short, close-fitting underwear (die Unterhose/die Schlüpfer). Der Brief means a letter.
Bureau	*His bureau has just enough room for him and a secretary.* A bureau is a desk with drawers (der Schreibtisch). Das Büro means an office.
Burst	*Rapunzel likes to burst her hair every day.* To burst is to explode (platzen). Bürsten means to brush.

Car

"Honey, maybe next time we should hire a stretch limo?"
A car is an automobile (das Auto).
Der Car means a coach or tour bus.

Chef

"I'm a bit scared of my chef."
A chef is a professional cook (der Koch, die Köchin).
Der Chef means a boss.

Confession

"For the last time, what is your confession?"
A confession is an admission of guilt (das Geständnis).
Die Konfession means a religious denomination.

Devout

Maggie likes her customers to be very devout.
Devout is very religious (andächtig).
Devot means submissive.

Dose

Little Heidi was so ill the doctor gave her a double dose.
A dose is a specific amount, usually of medicine (die Dosierung).
Die Dose means a can.

Engaged

"Well, I am a very engaged employee."
Engaged is to be betrothed to someone (verlobt).
Engagiert means dedicated.

Fabric

Sadly, Karl has to work in a very ugly fabric.
Fabric is cloth or textile (der Stoff).
Die Fabrik means a factory.

Formula

"Please complete this formula, sir."
A formula is a mathematical relationship, usually expressed in symbols (die Formel).
Das Formular means a form or questionnaire.

Gift	*I bought my mother-in-law a special gift for her birthday.* A gift is a present (das Geschenk). Das Gift means poison.
Gymnasium	*Four years at the local gymnasium didn't produce the results Markus expected.* A gymnasium is a sports hall (die Turnhalle). Das Gymnasium means a secondary school.
Herd	*Christina has a new ceramic herd in her kitchen.* A herd is a group of animals (die Herde). Der Herd means a stove or cooker.
Hose	*Jack needed a bigger hose.* A hose is a flexible tube for transporting liquid (der Schlauch). Die Hose means trousers.
Hut	*Beatrice always wears a hut when she is sunbathing.* A hut is a small structure, often made of wood (die Hütte). Der Hut means a hat.
Lager	*Once the lager was open, Bob and Ted couldn't leave.* A lager is a type of beer (helles Bier). Das Lager means a store or warehouse.
Lecture	*The children dreaded it being father's turn for the lecture at bedtime.* A lecture is a speech given to a class or formal audience (der Vortrag). Die Lektüre means a reading.
Loch	*Golf was invented in Scotland, which is why a golf course has 18 lochs.* A loch is a lake in Scotland (schottischer See). Das Loch means a hole.

Melon	*A British banker always used to wear a melon to work.* A melon is a type of fruit (die Melone). Die Melone also means a slang word for a bowler hat.
Menu	*"He ordered the WHOLE MENU!"* A menu is a restaurant's list of dishes served (die Speisekarte). Das Menü means a fixed price meal of two or three courses.
Middle-aged	*"This is our famous middle-aged fountain."* Middle-aged is somewhere between youth and old age (mittleren Alters). Mittelalterlich means medieval.
Mist	*He couldn't see anything in the mist.* A mist is a light fog (leichter Nebel). Der Mist means manure.
Old timer	*Doris loved polishing her old timer.* An old timer is slang for an old man (alter Hase). Der Oldtimer means a vintage car.
Pension	*Poor old John has a very small pension.* A pension is a regular income after retirement (die Rente) Die Pension is a guesthouse or small hotel
Pickle	*Teenage boys often suffer from pickles on their faces.* A pickle is a gherkin or pickled cucumber (die Essiggurke). Der Pickel means a spot or pimple.
Pregnant	*The key to being a successful salesman is to be pregnant.* Pregnant is to be expecting a baby (schwanger). Prägnant means concise.

Preservative	*"Preservatives help some things last longer."* A preservative is an additive that conserves food (der Konservierungsstoff). Der Präservativ means a condom.
Puff	*After two puffs he was out of breath.* A puff is a breath or exhalation (der Hauch). Der Puff means a brothel.
Rank	*Leo was tall, rank and handsome.* Rank is smelly or disgusting (stinkend). Rank means slim or slender.
Rat	*The depressed cat needed some rat.* A rat is a type of rodent (die Ratte). Der Rat means advice or a suggestion.
Roman	*Betty liked to take a Roman to bed with her.* A Roman is someone from Rome (der Römer, die Römerin). Der Roman is a novel.
Smoking	*"Sorry, sir, no smoking."* Smoking is the act of smoking a cigarette (das Rauchen). Der Smoking is a dinner jacket or tuxedo.
Stick	*They stick together.* To stick is to attach or adhere (kleben). Sticken is to embroider.
Tablet	*My wife gave me two tablets for my headache.* A tablet is a pill (die Tablette). Das Tablett is a tray.

Taste	*Peter loves to taste his new computer.* To taste is to try something by eating or licking it (schmecken). Tasten is to touch.
Treasure	*Blackbeard sat on his treasure to keep it safe.* A treasure is a collection of money and valuables (der Schatz). Der Tresor is a safe.
Turkey	*"Last year I went on holiday in the Turkey."* A turkey is a type of bird (der Truthahn). Die Türkei is the country Turkey, but in English without a 'the'.
Urn	*Swiss voters go to the urn every few months.* An urn is a vase or a container for holding the ashes after cremation (die Urne). Die Urne also means a ballot box.
Wand	*"Mirror, mirror on the wand..."* A wand is a magician's stick (der Zauberstab). Die Wand is a wall.
Wink	*The Queen always winks at the crowd.* To wink is to close one eye quickly (zwinkern). Winken is to wave.